DATE DUE		

3/10/2010 11:15 AM

BIO
CLINTON

33577000311694
Benson, Michael.

Bill Clinton

BILL
CLINTON

PRESIDENTIAL ✦ LEADERS

BILL CLINTON

MICHAEL BENSON

LERNER PUBLICATIONS COMPANY/MINNEAPOLIS

To Keith Brenner

Lerner Publications Company
A division of Lerner Publishing Group
241 First Avenue North
Minneapolis, MN 55401 U.S.A.

Website address: www.lernerbooks.com

Library of Congress Cataloging-in-Publication Data

Benson, Michael.
    Bill Clinton / by Michael Benson.
        p.   cm. — (Presidential leaders)
    Summary: Describes Bill Clinton's rise to the presidency, the ups and downs he experienced during his two terms in office, and his activities after his time in the White House.
    Includes bibliographical references (p. 105) and index.
    ISBN: 0–8225–0819–2 (lib. bdg.)
    1. Clinton, Bill, 1946– —Juvenile literature. 2. Presidents—United States—Biography— Juvenile literature. [1. Clinton, Bill, 1946– 2. Presidents.] I. Title. II. Series.
    E886.B46 2004
    973.929'092—dc21   2003003560

Manufactured in the United States of America
1 2 3 4 5 6 – JR – 09 08 07 06 05 04

CONTENTS

———— ✧ ————

INTRODUCTION 7

1 **A BOY BORN IN HOPE** 9

2 **COLLEGE YEARS** 17

3 **OXFORD** 27

4 **YALE LAW SCHOOL—ENTER HILLARY** 35

5 **THE GOVERNOR OF ARKANSAS** 45

6 **RUN FOR THE WHITE HOUSE** 59

7 **FIRST TERM** 67

8 **SECOND TERM** 75

9 **AT HOME IN HARLEM** 89

   TIMELINE 100

   SOURCE NOTES 103

   SELECTED BIBLIOGRAPHY 105

   FURTHER READING AND WEBSITES 106

   INDEX 108

Bill Clinton was sworn in as president in front of the U.S. Capitol in 1993.

INTRODUCTION

"We must provide for our nation the way a family provides for its children."
—Bill Clinton, first inaugural address, 1993

At age 46, Bill Clinton became the youngest man to be elected president of the United States since John F. Kennedy, who was elected in 1960 at the age of 43. Clinton was the first person born after World War II (1939–1945) to be elected to the nation's highest office. This made him the first member of the generation known as the baby boomers to make it to the White House.

In his inauguration speech on January 21, 1993, Clinton said:

> When our founders boldly declared America's independence to the world and our purposes to the Almighty, they knew that America, to endure, would have to change. Not change for change's sake, but change to preserve America's ideals—life, liberty, the pursuit of happiness.

Though we march to the music of our time, our mission is timeless. Each generation of Americans must define what it means to be an American. . . . We must do what no generation has had to do before. We must invest more in our own people, in their jobs, in their future, and at the same time cut our massive debt. We must do so in a world in which we must compete for every opportunity. It will not be easy; it will require sacrifice. But it can be done, and done fairly, not choosing the sacrifice for its own sake, but for our own sake.

Compassion, as always, was the key to Bill Clinton's policies.

Bill Clinton was the president of the United States, the commander in chief of the U.S. military, the leader of the Free World. One might think that Clinton was born in a rich family—with a silver spoon in his mouth, as they say—with all of the advantages that life can give. But nothing could be further from the truth. All of Bill Clinton's advantages were earned through hard work. He came from humble beginnings.

CHAPTER ONE

A BOY BORN IN HOPE

*"My grandparents had a lot to do with my
early commitment to learning. They taught
me to count and read. I was reading
little books when I was three."*
—Bill Clinton

In the early daylight hours of August 19, 1946, William Jefferson Blythe IV was born, one month prematurely, at Julia Chester Hospital in Hope, Arkansas, population 8,000. The name on his birth certificate reads William Jefferson Blythe IV.

He was named after his father, who had been killed in a one-car crash three months before his son was born. The baby future president would be raised by his mother and his grandparents.

When Bill was still a baby, his mother, Virginia, met a local businessman named Roger Clinton at her father's grocery store. Roger's nickname was "Dude," and he owned a car dealership in Hope. Two years later, Virginia Blythe moved to New Orleans for two years to study to be a nurse anesthetist. She needed a way to support herself and her small son.

During that time, Bill stayed with his grandparents in Hope. Bill's grandfather's general store served both black and white people. There were not many stores in Arkansas during the 1950s that could make that claim. It was through his grandfather, who taught him to respect people regardless of their color or religion, that Bill learned his lifelong hatred of racism and bigotry.

In 1950, when Bill was four, Virginia married Roger Clinton. From then on, Bill called Roger "Daddy," and that was how he thought of him. By first grade, Bill was known as Bill Clinton in school, although Roger, who was out most nights, never spent much time with Bill. Roger Clinton never officially adopted the boy either.

Donna Taylor, who went to kindergarten with Bill Clinton, remembers him when he was five: "Some people like to be with other children. He was like that. He was always right there. Almost obnoxious. He was in the center of everything."

When Bill was six, the Clintons moved from Hope to Hot Springs, Arkansas. When Bill was ten, Roger and Virginia had a son, Bill's half brother. They named him Roger Clinton Jr.

GOING TO CHURCH ALONE

Bill was religious as a child, even though his household was not. His grandparents had given him early training in the Bible, and later a devout housekeeper encouraged his

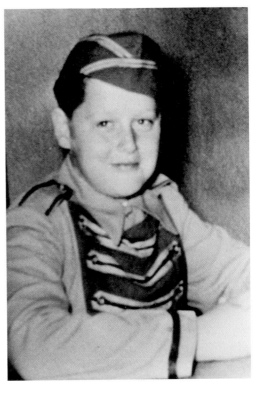

Bill, shown here in a band uniform, enjoyed playing his saxophone at concerts.

✧

churchgoing. At eight Bill would get himself up on Sunday mornings, put on his best suit and, carrying his Bible, walk the half mile to the Park Place Baptist Church.

In high school, Bill was an honor student and socially popular. He played the saxophone in a jazz band and was considered by many to be the best sax player in the city. He even competed to be named the best in the state. Clinton later wrote in a letter to a friend about his youth in Hot Springs: "No one ever enjoyed being kids more than we did—it would be pretty hard to crowd more living in."

TROUBLES AT HOME

His happy life at school, however, was countered by a not-so-pleasant life at home. Bill's stepfather was an alcoholic who became abusive when he was drunk. As Bill entered his teenage years, the elder Roger's drinking and violent behavior grew steadily worse. When Bill was fourteen years

As a teenager, Bill (left) was close to his mother and younger brother, and he was often protective of them.

———————————— ✧ ————————————

old, he finally told his stepfather that he'd had enough. Roger was not to lay a hand on his mother, his half brother, or himself ever again.

"If you want them, you'll have to go through me," Bill told his stepfather. By this time, the young man was already well over six feet tall. The abuse stopped, but Roger Clinton never did stop drinking.

By the time Bill was a teenager, he was acting more and more as the head of the household. He and his mother became closer in the adversity. She saw his promise and encouraged him to excel, and he protected her from his stepfather. Being head of the household was a role Bill adapted to easily. He had always seemed more mature than his age. Younger brother Roger adored him.

Virginia Clinton left her husband in the spring of 1962

and filed for divorce. Virginia was granted her divorce from Roger on May 15, 1962. Despite this, Bill had his name legally changed to William Jefferson Clinton so he and his brother Roger would have the same last name.

Bill later said that Virginia was a good role model for him. "She always worked; did a good job as a parent; and we had a lot of adversity in our life when I was growing up, and she handled it real well, and I think she gave me a high pain threshold, which, I think, is a very important thing to have in public life."

MEETING HIS HERO

During Bill Clinton's teen years, he wasn't always sure what he wanted to do with his life. Like many young people, he was still weighing his options, waiting to see which direction his life would take. For a time, he thought he might become a doctor or maybe a newspaper reporter. He was pretty good at playing the saxophone. The thought of becoming a professional musician even crossed his mind.

But all of that changed in June 1963. When Bill was a junior in high school, he was selected by his teachers to attend Arkansas Boys State, a summer session in government, at Camp Robinson in Little Rock, the capital of Arkansas. While attending that camp, Bill was elected camp senator. In his acceptance speech, the sixteen-year-old Clinton said, "It's the biggest thrill and honor of my life. I hope I can do a tremendous job required of me as a representative of the state. I hope I can live up to the task." The Boys State summer ended with Bill elected as an Arkansas representative to the American Legion's Boys Nation.

In a moment that set the direction of his life, awestruck Bill eagerly shook hands with President Kennedy.

THE HANDSHAKE

The Boys Nation group was invited to the White House Rose Garden to meet President John F. Kennedy, and Bill had the opportunity to shake hands with him. Bill claims he wasn't yet dreaming of becoming the president of the United States himself, but from that point on, he knew that he wanted to be in politics.

The handshake was not just a matter of good luck. When Bill got off the school bus at the White House, he rushed ahead so that he would be able to sit in the front row. That way he would be closest to the podium. When Kennedy was through with his speech, Clinton was the first to jump up to shake the president's hand.

A photograph was taken of the young Bill Clinton proudly shaking hands with President Kennedy. That photo seemed to say that Bill Clinton was destined for greatness.

On the same trip, Clinton had lunch with another of his heroes, J. William Fulbright, a Democratic senator from Arkansas. Fulbright was the longtime chairman of the Senate Foreign Relations Committee and the original sponsor of the Fulbright scholarships for international study. Clinton recalled: "Fulbright I admired to no end. . . . He had a real impact on my wanting to be a citizen of the world."

Many years later, as president, Clinton attended a tribute to Senator Fulbright, and he said, "People dumped on our state and said we were all a bunch of back country hayseeds, and we had a guy in the Senate who doubled the IQ of any room he entered. It was pretty encouraging. It made us feel pretty good, like we might amount to something." Fulbright, as it turned out, would remember the young Clinton and play an important part in Bill's future.

*As a freshman at Georgetown University, Bill showed an active
interest in government and politics.*

CHAPTER TWO

COLLEGE YEARS

"Hello, I'm Bill Clinton. Will you help me run for president of the class?"
—Bill Clinton, Georgetown University, 1964

Clinton graduated from high school near the top of his class—fourth in a class of 363. He was a member of the National Honor Society and a National Merit Scholarship semifinalist. Naturally, he wanted to be in Washington, D.C., where the U.S. government functions, so he applied to and was accepted at Georgetown University in Washington. Bill majored in international studies. He earned the money to pay for this expensive college by working in the office of Senator Fulbright, the man he had lunched with as a teenaged representative of Boys Nation. As Fulbright's aide, Bill became what was known as one of the "back-room boys." He did filing, clipped items out of newspapers, and ran errands between the Senate Office Building and the Capitol Building.

Active and friendly, Bill campaigned for student government at Georgetown.

———————— ✧ ————————

Clinton recalled: "I'd never been out of Arkansas really very much, and there I was with people from all over the country and all over the world." Despite the fact that he had a southern accent and sometimes felt like an outsider—being from Arkansas—Bill was just as popular as ever. He was big, and he liked to get close to people when he talked to them. He was a backslapping, shoulder-squeezing, hand-shaking kind of guy.

On October 30, 1964, he was elected the president of his freshmen class. Most of his fellow students were charmed by what seemed like Bill's hayseed enthusiasm.

TOO GOOD TO BE TRUE?

As would be true throughout Clinton's political career, there were those who thought Clinton's positive attitude was too good to be true. He was always social. He was always in a good mood. He was always enthusiastic. To put it simply, there were those who figured Bill Clinton just had to be a phony.

At Georgetown one of his political rivals realized that Clinton was very sensitive about this. When he called Clinton a fake in public, the young man's face turned red and he almost lost his temper. This kind of criticism didn't put the slightest dent in Bill's tremendous popularity, however. He was elected sophomore class president at the beginning of his second year at Georgetown.

PLEDGING A FRATERNITY

Bill pledged (joined) a fraternity during his sophomore year. It was Alpha Phi Omega, and it ran the campus elections. To get into the fraternity, he had to be initiated, which meant that he had to be the slave of a "Big Brother," who was already a member. Bill shined his Big Brother's shoes and allowed himself to be led around blindfolded, but he finally was an Alpha Phi Omega brother.

Some found the hazing, as this process of humiliation was known, of potential fraternity members to be uncivilized, but Bill cheerfully saw the symbolism of it all. As far as he was concerned, everything good was worth suffering for. Giving up was for losers.

During the summer of 1966, Bill got his first taste of a real-life political campaign. His friend Lyda Holt's father, Judge Frank Holt, was running for governor of Arkansas, and Bill helped with the campaign. While Bill was speaking on the judge's behalf, people began to notice his political skills. Lyda Holt recalls, "If we had any doubts about [Bill's] future, they were erased. He had that ability to take feelings and emotions and match them to words." Holt did not win the election, but many people recalled the tall young man who had given such moving speeches at rallies across Arkansas during the long campaign.

EYE ON HIS FUTURE

Clinton did not run for junior class president. He began working on his campaign for the student council president election at the end of his junior year. It was 1967, and most young people on college campuses across the nation were opposed to the war in Vietnam. They protested the draft (required enrollment in the U.S. army) and America's partic- ipation in the unpopular war. Clinton's campaign message

——————————— ✧ ———————————

Young Americans showed their opposition to the Vietnam War.

A *poster from Clinton's unsuccessful run for student council president* ──────────── ✧

A REALISTIC APPROACH TO STUDENT GOVERNMENT

BILL CLINTON

CANDIDATE

PRESIDENT OF THE STUDENT COUNCIL

of working together to change things seemed very "establishment" (traditional). The student body at Georgetown was "antiestablishment," and Clinton lost the election. After the election, Clinton said, "If I do it again, I'll just have to work harder. Instead of handbills under every door, I'll have to talk to everybody in person."

During the spring of his junior year, Clinton learned that his stepfather, Roger, who had since remarried Bill's mother, had cancer. The only father Bill had ever known passed away during November of Bill's senior year, with Virginia, Bill, and Roger Jr. at his side. Bill had come to understand alcoholism, the disease from which his stepfather suffered, and he was able to forgive him for the abuses he had had to endure.

LUCKY BREAK

Losing the election for student council president at Georgetown turned out to be a lucky break for Bill Clinton. He had more time than he thought he would, and he decided to compete for a Rhodes Scholarship, one of the most prestigious awards a student in America can win. Senator Fulbright encouraged Bill to apply.

Despite his academic achievements, Bill was not considered by many to be a likely candidate for a Rhodes Scholarship. The scholarship selection committee had a reputation for rewarding athleticism as well as academics. But Bill was not a jock. After applying for the scholarship, Bill took up jogging several miles a day in hopes that it would give him a more athletic appearance. As it turned out, Clinton breezed through the Rhodes Scholarship selection process despite his relative clumsiness in the gym.

During Bill's senior year, friends reported he had become heavily critical of the war in Vietnam. The U.S. bombing of civilians in North Vietnamese cities made him wonder what our nation's values were supposed to be. He also became increasingly vocal about civil rights. With so much focus on the war, he realized that America was losing its commitment to protecting the right of everyone to be treated equally and fairly.

THE DRAFT

On February 16, 1968, while Bill was a senior at Georgetown, President Richard Nixon declared that students enrolled in graduate school—with the exception of medical students—would no longer be exempt from the military draft. At the time, the draft law stated that any American man over the age of eighteen could be called up at any time to enter the military service for a minimum of two years. Without the draft, the U.S. army had trouble finding enough soldiers to fight wars. Draftees went into the army as privates.

Newly drafted young men wait for their military papers to be processed.

Bill knew if he were drafted, he would end up an army private, perhaps on a path that might lead to Vietnam. In Vietnam U.S. troops were fighting an escalating war that was little understood by most Americans. Bill wondered if he should use his ever-growing list of political connections to find a way around the draft law. Clinton agonized over his choices. The problem became more pressing as his attitudes about the unpopular war changed—and each time he heard of an old friend coming back from Vietnam in a coffin.

Civil rights leader Martin Luther King Jr. and Senator Robert Kennedy, a presidential candidate and brother of

*National Guard soldiers entered a Washington, D.C., neighborhood
to try to control arson and looting during an April 1968 riot.*

President John F. Kennedy, were both assassinated in 1968.
In response to their deaths, African American neighborhoods across America erupted in riots during the spring
and summer of that year. Clinton signed up with the Red
Cross and delivered food and supplies to Washington's riot-
torn inner city.

Robert Kennedy's assassination took place five days
before Clinton's graduation from Georgetown. Kennedy's
death seemed to loom over what should have been a happy
moment in his life, much as the assassination of President
John F. Kennedy had haunted Clinton's senior year in high
school. Because of Robert Kennedy's death, Clinton's
Georgetown graduation ceremony was expected to be a

somber affair. A thunderstorm at the beginning of the commencement speech canceled the outdoor ceremonies entirely. Even so, Bill Clinton became the first member of his family to graduate from college.

Following graduation, Clinton went back to work for Senator Fulbright, this time working full time on Fulbright's reelection committee. Bill had to leave Fulbright's campaign before the election, though. It was time for him to head to Oxford University in England on the Rhodes Scholarship he had been awarded.

Clinton (center) was one of more than thirty male college graduates from the United States who were given the honor of studying at Oxford.

CHAPTER THREE

OXFORD

"Being in England was incredible. I got to travel a lot. I got to spend a lot of personal time—learn things, go see things. I read about three hundred books both years I was there."
—Bill Clinton

The Rhodes Scholarship was founded in 1902 and is the oldest international scholarship in the world. Cecil J. Rhodes, a British colonial pioneer and statesman, set up the program in his will. The will listed the criteria for winners. It said that Rhodes scholars must have "literary and scholastic attainments; the energy to use their talents to the full, as exemplified by fondness for and success in sports; truth, courage, devotion to duty, sympathy for and protection of the weak, kindliness, unselfishness, and fellowship; moral force of character and instincts to lead, and an interest in one's fellow beings." Rhodes's idea was to bring outstanding students from other countries to study free of cost for two

Cecil J. Rhodes

————— ◆ —————

years at England's Oxford University. Oxford is one of the oldest and most distinguished universities in the world.

The first honorees from the United States were named in 1904. Since then, thirty-two Rhodes Scholarships, four each from eight districts, are awarded each year to American college seniors. Until 1976 this meant men only. After that, women were also eligible. The scholarship was designed to provide special educational opportunities to future world leaders—and this certainly could not have been truer than when Bill Clinton was a recipient—and to promote international understanding.

SAILING THE ATLANTIC

In October Clinton boarded the S.S. *United States* at Pier 86 on the Hudson River in New York City. With him were his fellow American scholarship winners. Sailing the Atlantic Ocean was a Rhodes Scholarship tradition.

The journey gave the winners a chance to get to know one another, and Clinton made a solid impression on the others. One said, "He was an extraordinary listener." Another said, "I remember meeting Clinton and him telling me within 45 minutes that he planned to go back to Arkansas to be governor or senator and would like to be a national leader someday."

Also aboard the ship was Bobby Baker, a friend of former U.S. president Lyndon Johnson. Baker was traveling to Europe to escape a political scandal. While the other Rhodes scholars scorned Baker, Clinton spent much time talking to him, picking his brain for his knowledge of the inner workings of the Washington power structure.

At journey's end, the ship dropped off the scholars at Southampton, on the southern coast of England. They were met by the former British chief of intelligence during World War II, Sir Edgar Williams. He escorted them by bus to the dark stone buildings of the Oxford campus.

ANCIENT SURROUNDINGS

Oxford was old. The college Bill attended dated back to one King Alfred had built in the year 872. In America, during Clinton's Oxford years, campuses were torn by riots as anti-Vietnam protests got out of hand. But in the medieval campus of Oxford, the atmosphere remained quiet. Continuing his new concentration on athletics, Bill took up the sport of rugby, which is a cross between soccer and American football. He even joined the school's subvarsity basketball team.

Decades later Clinton would cause a controversy by admitting that he had once "experimented with marijuana" at Oxford but that he "didn't inhale." The story struck many as preposterous, but those who knew Clinton during his Oxford years say that his story is the truth.

In January 1969, Clinton traveled back to Arkansas because his mother was getting married again. His arrival

Oxford University, located about fifty miles northwest of London, is made up of thirty-nine separate colleges.

was kept a surprise, and Virginia later said everyone was lucky she didn't have a heart attack when Clinton showed up. Clinton had grown a beard and wore his hair long, as was popular among the antiwar youth of America. Later that same month, back in England, he had the physical examination required by the draft laws at a U.S. air base near London. It was determined that he was physically fit to serve in the military.

During the spring break of his first year at Oxford, Clinton traveled with a group of friends to Germany. There he went ice skating for the first time and visited many snowy villages.

DRAFTED

On April 30, 1969, the number of U.S. military personnel in Vietnam peaked at more than five hundred thousand. That same day, Clinton received a letter in England from his local draft board in Arkansas. He had been drafted. At the end of Clinton's first year at Oxford, his friends, convinced that he was army bound and would not be returning, threw a farewell party that, it is said, lasted three days.

Back in the United States, waiting to be called into service, Clinton enrolled at the University of Arkansas Law School. The university had an ROTC (Reserve Officers Training Corps) program that was considered by the draft board to be an acceptable alternative military service.

During the Vietnam era, 26.8 million men in America were of an appropriate age to serve in the military. Of these, 2.2 million were drafted. Another 8.7 million enlisted in— that is, voluntarily joined—the U.S. armed services during that same period. Many graduate students who disapproved of the war were looking for loopholes to get out of military service. Sixteen million of those men managed to avoid the draft, mostly through legal means. Only 209,000 of those avoiding the draft were ever arrested as draft dodgers, and of those, only 8,750 were convicted.

THE ANTIWAR CLINTON

Clinton was not scheduled to start his ROTC program until the summer of 1970, so he returned to Oxford for his second year. But his mind was not on his studies. He stopped attending class regularly and became, for a brief period, a full-time antiwar organizer working with a group called the Vietnam Moratorium Committee.

*Members of the Vietnam Moratorium Committee demonstrated against
U.S. involvement in the war in Vietnam.*

———————— ✧ ————————

In his role as an organizer, Clinton helped arrange peaceful protests against the war in Vietnam. One protest he organized involved several hundred American students standing out in front of the U.S. Embassy in London holding burning candles.

After a semester involved in antiwar organizing, Clinton became a serious student once again for the second term of his second year. He even signed up for an additional "cram course" to help him make up for lost time. Clinton's ability to excel in academics, while maintaining a poor attendance record in his classes, is evidence that he was a quick study. When he wanted to, he could learn things very rapidly.

Clinton did not earn a degree during his two years at Oxford, but he did learn a great deal about England and the rest of Europe. Many Rhodes scholars left Oxford without a graduate degree. Students were encouraged to shape the experience to cover their own needs rather than to the requirements of earning a degree.

During his time at Oxford, Clinton had traveled in western Europe and to the Communist countries of eastern Europe. In Moscow, the capital of the Soviet Union, he hung out and drank coffee with other Americans for a few days and then traveled to Prague, the capital city of

——————————— ◇ ———————————

During part of his second year at Oxford, Clinton (center) lived with two American friends, Strobe Talbott (left) and Frank Aller (right).

Czechoslovakia (present-day Czech Republic). As his time at Oxford came to an end, Clinton wrote a letter to the head of the ROTC program at the University of Arkansas and explained that he would not be going there as expected. Since his application, he explained, he had become a full-fledged antiwar protester with no interest in ROTC.

Clinton's next step was to apply to Yale Law School, a more highly respected school than the University of Arkansas. Yale was a school that would look just right on Clinton's resume when he ran for his first public office.

CHAPTER FOUR

YALE LAW SCHOOL— ENTER HILLARY

"He was one guy who wasn't afraid of me. . . . He cared deeply about where he came from, which was unusual. He was rooted and most of us were disconnected."
—Hillary Rodham Clinton

Clinton entered Yale in the autumn of 1970 but did not immediately start going to class. As usual, politics was the cause of the distraction. Instead of focusing on law school, he helped run the U.S. Senate campaign of Joseph D. Duffey, a peace and civil rights activist in Connecticut. Duffey lost the election.

Clinton showed up for class in November, asking if he could borrow someone's notes. As it turned out, he didn't need long to catch up. He had no difficulty passing his first-year law courses.

At Yale Law School, a young woman in Clinton's class

caught his attention. One day, when he was staring at her with a dreamy expression on his face, she approached him. She said, "Look, if you're going to keep staring at me and I'm going to be staring back, we might as well know each other. I'm Hillary Rodham. What's your name?" Clinton later said, "It turned out she knew who I was, but I didn't know that at the time. But I was real impressed." They were in a number of classes together, and Hillary was the better student.

On their first outing—it wasn't really a date—they went for a walk and came up with the idea of touring the campus art museum. They were momentarily disappointed when they discovered the museum was closed.

Prestigious Yale Law School, located in New Haven, Connecticut, was founded in 1824.

HILLARY RODHAM

Hillary Diane Rodham was born in Chicago, Illinois, on October 26, 1947, and grew up in Park Ridge, a Chicago suburb. Hillary was the oldest of three children—she has a pair of younger brothers, Hugh and Tony.

Growing up, her interests were sports and politics. While in grade school, Hillary wrote to NASA, the National Aeronautics and Space Administration, to inquire about becoming an astronaut when she grew up. But the form letter she received discouraged girls from applying. In those days, astronauts were all men.

Hillary was an excellent student. In high school, she was named to the National Honor Society and graduated from high school in the top five percent of her class. Her senior yearbook proclaimed her Most Likely to Succeed.

In 1965 Hillary entered Wellesley College in Massachusetts and graduated with high honors. She represented her college several times on the television quiz show *G.E. College Bowl* and won.

Hillary took after her father and was politically conservative as a young girl. As she grew older, she developed her own moderate to sometimes strongly liberal point of view.

———————————— ✦

Hillary (front, center) *served on her high school's student council. She is shown here in her yearbook with fellow members of the group.*

But Clinton was not to be denied. He got the attention of a janitor inside the museum and talked him into letting Hillary and him in. In exchange for the after-hours admission, the couple agreed to pick up some trash.

Hillary got another inkling that Clinton was interested in her when they went together to sign up for second semester classes and waited in a long line. When they got to the front of the line, Hillary learned that Clinton didn't need to register. He had done it the day before.

AN UNBEATABLE TEAM

As their romance bloomed, the couple found that they made a good pair in class as well. In law school, students learn how to work in trials by participating in something called moot court. In moot court, students work on made-up cases that are tried as if they were real, with the teacher as the judge. Clinton and Hillary were an unbeatable team when they combined forces in moot court. They had contrasting but complimentary styles. He was country charm, and she was urban efficiency. He was emotional. She was rational and calm. They were so good at trying cases in moot court that they competed in and won campuswide moot court tournaments.

The summer after his first year of law school, Clinton went to Texas to help with the 1972 Democratic presidential campaign of George McGovern there. Senator McGovern was running against the nation's Republican president, Richard Nixon. The fact that McGovern was not very popular in Texas did not dampen Clinton's enthusiasm. While campaigning he gained many important contacts that would serve him well later in his political life.

*Candidate McGovern greeted supporters. The U.S. senator from
South Dakota ran for president on an antiwar platform.*

———————— ✧ ————————

Hillary went to Texas also. She took a job with
the Democratic National Committee, getting potential
Democrats to register to vote in Austin, Texas. She was able
to see Clinton all the time. After Hillary had left Texas and
returned to Yale for the start of the fall semester, Clinton
stayed on to work for the campaign to the bitter end. In
November Nixon received more than two-thirds of the vote
in Texas and won a nationwide landslide victory.

For the second year in a row, Clinton showed up late for
school and had to play catch-up. As was true during his first
year, he had no trouble passing any of that semester's classes.

CLINTON THE TEACHER

After receiving his law degree in 1973, Clinton, just twenty-seven, became a teacher at the University of Arkansas Law School in Fayetteville. With his youth, charisma, and natural speaking ability, Professor Clinton quickly became one of the most popular teachers at the school. He was also an easy grader. In a school where 30 percent of the first-year students failed, Professor Clinton never failed anybody. In fact, he rarely gave a grade lower than a B.

But his popularity went deeper than just his kindness at report-card time. He was also completely open-minded concerning race. He didn't care what color a person was, a trait that set him apart and made him extremely popular with his African American students.

At the time Clinton was teaching at the University of Arkansas, the student body had only recently been integrated. Before that, African Americans had been unable to attend the whites-only school. The black students at the university, when Clinton taught there, were among the first African Americans to attend. Clinton understood the social difficulties facing those black students as they dealt with ongoing discrimination from many of their teachers as well as the white student body. He went out of his way to help them succeed.

FIRST RUN FOR POLITICAL OFFICE

On February 25, 1974, Clinton began his own political career. He ran for U.S. Congress, in hopes of representing the Third District in Arkansas, an area that covered twenty-one counties within the state.

Clinton made the announcement in Hot Springs, before

about sixty friends and family. His mother, Virginia, was at the announcement and was seen grinning broadly, telling everyone how proud she was of her son.

Clinton's opponent during the campaign was a popular Republican, John Paul Hammerschmidt. Hammerschmidt had earned a whopping seventy-seven percent of the vote in the previous election. Hammerschmidt seemed impossible to beat. But Clinton was tireless. He went from town to town, determined to personally shake the hand and ask for the vote of every resident of his district.

While Clinton was running for office, Hillary Rodham was in Washington. She was one of thirty-nine lawyers assigned to build a case for impeachment (charging an official with misconduct while in office) against President Nixon. During Nixon's reelection campaign, members of his staff had ordered a break-in at Democratic National Party headquarters in the Watergate Hotel in Washington, D.C. The burglars were looking for information on Democratic campaign plans. When they were caught, Nixon ordered that all connections between

Nixon's successes as president in international affairs were overshadowed by his involvement in the Watergate scandal.

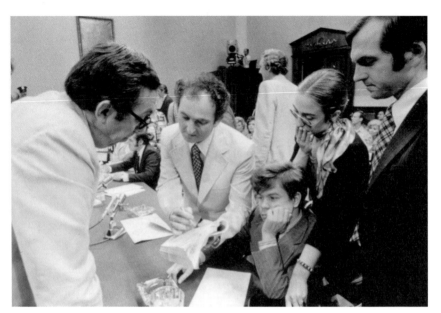

Hillary and other lawyers investigated the possibility of impeaching President Nixon.

his administration and those involved with the break-in be covered up. The cover-up and other illegal activities associated with it became known as the Watergate scandal. The investigation into the scandal was cut short when Nixon resigned rather than face impeachment.

Following Nixon's resignation, Hillary went to Arkansas and, like her future husband, took a job as a teacher at the University of Arkansas Law School. Her style—strict, inflexible, and in your face—couldn't have been more different from Clinton's.

Hillary arrived in time to take part in the final months of Clinton's campaign for Congress. It took a while for Clinton's friends and supporters in Arkansas to get used to

Hillary. With her direct personality and a Chicago accent, she seemed to be strictly business.

Though he lost the election, Clinton earned more votes than had any other Democrat in that district in twenty-five years. The margin of victory had been just six thousand votes. Losing an election is usually damaging to a candidate's political future, but that was not the case for Clinton. Because of his youth and his unexpectedly strong showing in his first election, his future looked bright. Clinton was a rising star.

Clinton did not waste any time sulking in the aftermath of defeat. By the morning following the election, he was already back on the sidewalks of Arkansas, greeting people and shaking hands, getting ready for the next campaign.

WEDDING BELLS

The following year, on October 11, 1975, Clinton and Hillary married. The traditional Methodist wedding took place in the living room of the house he had bought for them in Fayetteville.

Hillary and Clinton's mother, Virginia, were slow to get along. Virginia had decided that her son should marry a southern woman. Hillary was a no-nonsense northerner, and her manner never radiated southern-style charm. She further irritated Virginia by refusing to be known as Mrs. Clinton. Her name, even after she was married, was to be Hillary Rodham.

Clinton showed off his musical talent at a party celebrating his 1979 inauguration as governor of Arkansas.

CHAPTER FIVE

THE GOVERNOR
OF ARKANSAS

"We must dedicate more of our limited resources to paying our teachers better; expanding educational opportunities in poor and small school districts . . . and strengthening basic education."
—Bill Clinton, gubernatorial inauguration address, 1979

Clinton's next run for political office came in 1976, as he was about to turn thirty. He took a leave of absence from the University of Arkansas to run for attorney general of Arkansas. The former attorney general, the top lawyer in the state, had resigned to run for Congress. Clinton had a fairly easy time in the primary against two other Democratic hopefuls. The Republicans did not even come up with a candidate, so Clinton ran unopposed. At the same time, Clinton directed the Arkansas presidential

Clinton met with presidential candidate Carter,
another Democrat from the South.

────────────── ◇ ──────────────

campaign of Georgia governor Jimmy Carter. Hillary left
Arkansas temporarily and went to Indiana to direct that
state's Carter campaign.

That fall Jimmy Carter defeated the Republican nominee,
President Gerald Ford, and Clinton was elected Arkansas's
attorney general. He appointed Hillary chairperson of
Arkansas's Legal Services Corporation. This corporation is a
Washington-based nonprofit organization that makes sure poor
people facing legal trouble get proper legal representation.

Clinton endeared himself to the people of Arkansas during his time as attorney general. He worked to keep utilities
(power companies) from raising rates and relieved over-
crowding in the prisons. He transformed the Old State

House in Little Rock into a thriving modern museum. After he had been attorney general for a year, the time seemed right for his next career move. In 1978 he announced he would run for governor of Arkansas.

During his campaign for governor, both Clinton and his wife were heavily criticized. Hillary had to put up with some people's mistrust of powerful women and lawyers. Clinton had to overcome rumors that he was a draft dodger because he had backed out of his ROTC commitment at the University of Arkansas. The criticism didn't slow the campaign down much, however. Clinton won the Democratic nomination during the summer of 1978, with 60 percent of the vote, and won the election in November, with 63 percent of the vote. He became the youngest governor in the United States since the 1930s.

With Hillary at his side, Clinton was sworn in as one of the youngest governors in U.S. history.

IMPROVING EDUCATION

The Clintons moved into the governor's mansion in Little Rock. As governor, Clinton's first concern was with improving the school system in Arkansas, which ranked as one of the worst in the country. Part of the reason that Arkansas schools functioned so poorly was that they were financially poor. Arkansas residents paid less in tax money for education than most other states. In order to improve schools, Clinton realized, more money was going to have to be spent—and that meant he was going to have to raise taxes.

More money for education was only part of Clinton's ambitious plan. He also wanted to require Arkansas schoolteachers to take a test to prove their competency in teaching skills. He also wanted to streamline the state's school system, which was divided into many small, poor, rural districts. Much of his plan never was accomplished because the state senate refused to approve the necessary tax hike.

Clinton also wanted to improve the state's road system, a system that still had dirt roads in a time when other states were building superhighways. And he wanted to protect the air, water, and land from pollution. Citizens of Arkansas probably felt that their new young governor was trying to do too much all at once. Again and again, Clinton found that the people of his state were unwilling to pay for the improvements he was suggesting.

BIRTH OF CHELSEA

Hillary became pregnant in 1979, and on February 27, 1980—seventeen days before she was expected—Chelsea Victoria Clinton was born. Clinton intended to be in the birthing room when his daughter was born. But Hillary had difficulty during labor, and Chelsea was delivered by Caesarian section. Chelsea was beautiful and healthy, and Hillary quickly recovered from the birth. The family was doing well, but politically things were not looking good for Clinton.

REELECTION BID

Governor Clinton was receiving heavy criticism in the press. Some newspapers said he was too young and politically inexperienced to handle the responsibilities given to him. His bid for reelection did not go well. Every bad thing that had happened in Arkansas during his term was blamed on him. For example, during Clinton's first term, Cuban premier Fidel Castro had sent thousands of people, many of them convicts, out of Cuba. Most of those refugees had been settled at a military base in Arkansas, straining the state's resources and causing a furor among the locals. Clinton pleaded with President Jimmy Carter to make other states share the burden created by the refugees, but he was ignored. Clinton ended up taking the blame for the Cuban refugee problem, despite the fact that he had done nothing to cause it and had done his best to fix it.

Once again his critics were harsh on Hillary, as well. They hammered away at the fact that she refused to take her husband's name. In 1980 Clinton became the youngest governor ever to lose his bid for reelection.

The new governor was Republican Frank White. It wasn't long, however, before the voters of Arkansas regretted voting Clinton out of office. Governor White proved to be an inept chief, who once admitted to signing a bill into law without even reading it first.

Out of office, Clinton had to look for work. He took a job at the Little Rock law firm of Wright, Lindsey & Jennings. He tried to keep a positive attitude, but those close to him could tell that Clinton was bored with his job. His duties didn't involve politics, and politics had always been the one thing that drove him to action.

With White struggling as governor, Clinton sensed an opportunity and decided to run for governor once again. He announced his candidacy in February 1982, saying that he had learned from his mistakes. This time, he promised, he would listen more closely to the will of the people before acting. And this time, Clinton's critics had one less target. Hillary agreed to be known as Mrs. Bill Clinton— although when questioned by reporters, she admitted that she had not legally changed her name.

Clinton won the Democratic nomination for governor of Arkansas in 1982 with 54 percent of the vote. Polls showed that Clinton's popularity among African Americans was stronger than ever.

✧ ——————————
Two-year-old Chelsea, wearing a Clinton campaign button, helped out with her father's third run for governor.

Clinton supporters passed out stickers like this one during Clinton's gubernatorial campaign.
——————————— ✧

A SLIGHTLY DELAYED SECOND TERM

The Republicans nominated Governor White to run for reelection despite his poor performance in office, and Clinton was easily reelected governor of Arkansas in 1982. It was the first time ever that an Arkansas governor who had lost his bid for reelection was later elected again.

Clinton was sworn into office in Little Rock on January 11, 1983. His staff this time around was older and more experienced. Hillary took a leave of absence at the Rose Law Firm, where she had been hired as a lawyer, and went to work for her husband. With his wife at the head of his committee on educational standards, Governor Clinton successfully began the reform of the Arkansas school system. A law was passed stating that all teachers, not just the newly hired ones, had to pass a test in order to teach.

CONVENTION SPEECH

During the summer of 1984, Governor Clinton was invited to deliver a speech at the Democratic National Convention in San Francisco, California. This was the convention that would nominate Walter Mondale as the Democratic candidate for president. During the speech, Clinton rekindled

FIRST LADY OF ARKANSAS

While Clinton served as governor, Hillary continued her work for children and families as the first lady of the state. She chaired the Arkansas Education Standards Committee, and she founded the Arkansas Advocates for Children and Families. She introduced a program called Arkansas Home Instruction for Preschool Youth, teaching parents how to teach their preschool children to read.

She was named Arkansas Woman of the Year in 1983 and Arkansas Mother of the Year in 1984. Hillary was first lady of Arkansas for twelve years.

As part of her work to help young children, Hillary visited an Arkansas kindergarten class.

the words and ideas of the popular Democratic president Harry Truman.

Clinton said, "Harry Truman [if he were here today] would tell us to forget about 1948 and stand for what America needs in 1984. That's the way to attract millions of Americans who feel locked out and won't vote because they think we're irrelevant. That's the way to attract millions more, mostly young and

Harry Truman was president from 1945 to 1953.

well-educated, who intend to vote against us because they believe we have no plan for the future. Harry Truman would say: America has a productivity problem. What are we going to do about it? America is getting its brains beaten out in international economic competition. What are we going to do about it? America has millions of people who want to work but whose jobs have been lost because of competition from low wages abroad or the necessity to automate at home. What are we going to do about it?"

That same year, 1984, Clinton's political future was again thrown into crisis, this time because his younger brother, Roger, was arrested on serious drug charges. Instead of distancing himself from his brother, as another politician might have, Clinton was supportive of Roger and saw to it that he got medical help and good legal representation.

Clinton, Virginia, and Hillary were all in the courtroom

VERNOR
UGHES
aryland

GOVERNOR
GALLEN
New Hampshi

Clinton attended this meeting of the National Governors Association.
His participation allowed him to make valuable political connections.

in January 1985, showing family unity, when Roger was sentenced to two years in prison. Politically, Bill Clinton was never held accountable for Roger's crimes.

During this time, there were rumors in Arkansas that the Clintons were having problems with their marriage. People said that Clinton was seeing other women. Many women were attracted to the good-looking, young governor, and he enjoyed the attention.

A NATIONAL FIGURE

In 1986 Clinton became chairman of an organization known as the National Governors Association (NGA). This position gave Clinton more national visibility, which would help when he ran for national office. It gave him a forum to talk about things he wanted to accomplish, such as changes in the welfare system, the creation of jobs, and improving schools. Clinton also increased his visibility outside of Arkansas by delivering as many speeches as he could during his many trips on behalf of the NGA. Many of Clinton's friends and associates wanted him to run for president in 1988, but Clinton told them he thought Chelsea was too young, at eight, to handle the pressures of a presidential campaign—not to mention those of being the first daughter.

NOMINATING DUKAKIS

On July 20, 1988, Bill Clinton was to give the most important speech of his political career. He was asked to give the speech nominating the Democratic candidate for president, Michael Dukakis, at the Democratic Party's national convention in Atlanta, Georgia. This speech was designed to launch him into the national eye, and it served that function, but not in the way that Clinton had hoped.

It came very close to being the speech that ended Clinton's bright political future.

The speech was far too long. The delegates, eager to start the party that came after a candidate was nominated, were impatient

————————— ✧

Presidential candidate Michael Dukakis served as governor of Massachusetts for three terms.

Even though his speech at the Democratic convention in 1988 went badly, Clinton managed to look cheerful as he nominated Dukakis for president.

with Clinton and began to chant, "We want Mike [Dukakis]!" To those watching on TV, it was all too clear that no one was listening to Clinton.

Even with the crowd turning on him, Clinton did not cut the speech short. He continued on until the bitter end. When he said, "In conclusion," the crowd let loose with a mock cheer—much like the one a baseball pitcher gets when he throws his first strike after walking the bases loaded. In the convention hall, the speech had been embarrassing. On television it had appeared even worse—as if the gathered delegates were purposefully humiliating the governor of Arkansas.

THE TONIGHT SHOW

The day after Clinton's nominating speech, Johnny Carson, the host of *The Tonight Show,* made fun of it. But Clinton did not allow the embarrassing moments to hurt him. The next night, Clinton went on *The Tonight Show* in person, made jokes about the speech himself, and then entertained the crowd by playing a saxophone solo for America.

The appearance on Carson's show helped Clinton far more than the speech at the convention had hurt him. After all, Johnny Carson was watched by more people each night than had watched the Democratic convention. Clinton's reputation as a boring speechmaker continued, but he quickly proved not to be a boring person. "You have a good sense of humor," Carson said to Clinton on that show—and much of America agreed.

That year Michael Dukakis was soundly defeated by George H. W. Bush, a former U.S. ambassador, who had served as director of the Central Intelligence Agency (CIA). Four years later, President Bush would run for reelection, and this time his opponent would be the governor of Arkansas, Bill Clinton.

Clinton had been contemplating a presidential run for years.
In 1992 he realized his ambitions.

CHAPTER SIX

RUN FOR THE WHITE HOUSE

"I stand here today, because I refuse to stand by and let our children become part of the first generation to do worse than their parents."
—Bill Clinton, presidential candidacy
announcement speech, 1991

When Clinton ran again for reelection to a fifth term as governor of Arkansas, the voters were worried that he would abandon them to run for president in 1992. Clinton earned the trust and vote of the people of Arkansas by promising that, if he were reelected, he would serve a full term.

It was clear that Bill Clinton wanted to become president of the United States. The only real question was when would he run? Most of Clinton's closest associates, including Hillary, had sensed that he was becoming bored with the governor's job and were surprised when he ran again. Soon after being elected, though, he changed his mind and decided to seek the presidential nomination in 1992, despite his promise.

Clinton toured the state to see how the people in Arkansas felt about his running for president, and he learned that his followers were angry at him for breaking his promise. At the same time, many of them wanted very much to see him become president. Clinton made the people of Arkansas proud of their home state, just as Senator Fulbright had done before him. Clinton officially announced himself as a candidate for president on October 3, 1991.

Clinton made the announcement on the front steps of the Old State House in Little Rock. Standing on a platform flanked by twelve American flags, he told the cheering crowd: "The country is headed in the wrong direction fast, slipping behind, losing our way." As she listened to her son announcing his candidacy, Virginia knew that she was dying of cancer—but she had not yet told her sons of her condition.

———————————— ✧ ————————————

In front of a supportive crowd, Clinton announced his presidential candidacy in 1991 with considerable fanfare.

At the Democratic National Convention, attendees celebrated wildly at the news of Clinton's nomination.

ENTER AL GORE

Clinton received the Democratic Party's nomination for president at the 1992 national convention in New York City's Madison Square Garden. There he named as his vice-presidential running mate Al Gore of Tennessee, a forty-four-year-old senator with political beliefs much like his own.

Clinton had two opponents during the campaign. His Republican opponent was then-president George H. W. Bush. He also had to face H. Ross Perot, a Texas billionaire who was running for president as an independent—that is, without the backing of one of the two major political parties. It was clear from the start that the Perot campaign was

ALBERT GORE JR.

Clinton's vice-presidential running mate, Albert Gore Jr., was destined to become a politician. The son of Tennessee senator Albert Gore Sr. was born on March 31, 1948, in Washington, D.C. At a young age, he became familiar with the ways of political power.

Young Al felt as if he had two hometowns when he was growing up: Carthage, Tennessee, where his family lived, and Washington, D.C., where his father worked. Gore's favorite place was his family's farm in Carthage, where there were "horses and canoes and all the outdoors, where you know everybody and everybody knows you."

Gore attended St. Albans School for Boys in Washington, D.C. He earned a bachelor's degree in government at Harvard, graduating in 1969.

Though Gore was personally against the war in Vietnam, he enlisted in the army after he graduated from Harvard. He served in Vietnam as a reporter for the army newspaper *Stars and Stripes*. After his stint in the army, he took a job at a daily newspaper, the *Nashville Tennessean*, while attending Vanderbilt Law School at night.

Gore was elected to the U.S. House of Representatives in 1976. He served four terms in Congress, followed by two terms as senator from Tennessee. Gore was in Congress during the Cold War, a period of hostility between the United States and the Soviet Union when both nations were building increasing numbers of nuclear weapons. Gore became an expert on how to rid the world of nuclear arms. He also was interested in the preservation of the environment.

Gore ran for president in 1988. He lost the Democratic nomination that year to Michael Dukakis, who was defeated by George H. W. Bush.

At a presidential debate, Clinton compared his political views with those of his two opponents, George H. W. Bush (left) and Ross Perot (middle).

going to help Clinton more than it helped Bush. Perot attracted voters who would otherwise have voted for a Republican.

During Clinton's presidential campaign, he promised to take strong measures to strengthen the economy. He was going to cut taxes for ordinary people. He was going to completely reform American health care. Clinton believed that no one should be refused the medical care they needed because they could not afford it.

The campaign was marred by the statements of a woman named Gennifer Flowers, who claimed, with some proof, that she'd had a sexual relationship with Clinton during the time he was governor of Arkansas. Clinton and his wife appeared on national television together, and Clinton admitted that he had done some things that had brought "pain upon his marriage." During that TV appearance, he said of his marriage, "We never wanted to give up on each other and we still don't." After the interview, polls showed that the American public was not overly concerned with Clinton's reported misdeeds.

Clinton's selection of Gore as vice-presidential nominee had broken several political rules. It had always been considered wise to choose a running mate from a different geographical area, who had different views. A diverse ticket appeals to a broader base of people. Clinton chose Gore,

Both southerners in their mid-forties, Clinton and Gore had many political similarities.

who was nearly identical in his political philosophy and who was also from the South. But it worked. With a popular vice-presidential candidate and the success of Clinton's TV interview with Hillary, the Clinton-Gore ticket defeated President George H. W. Bush and Vice President Dan Quayle in 1992. Clinton won 43 percent of the vote, compared to 38 percent for Bush and 19 percent for Perot. Clinton was only the second Democrat in twenty-eight years to be elected president.

The Clintons looked to their years in the White House with optimism.

CHAPTER SEVEN

FIRST TERM

"I will stay up late and get up early and work hard as long as it takes to turn this country around and give it back to the American people."
—Bill Clinton, inaugural address, 1993

As soon as Clinton entered the White House, he set about to keep his campaign promises. To strengthen the economy and balance the budget, he called for almost $500 billion in tax increases and governmental spending cuts. Republicans were opposed to the increases, but the Democratic-controlled Congress gave President Clinton most of what he wanted.

One of Clinton's early successes was the Brady Bill, a law that requires customers to wait for five days before finalizing the purchase of a handgun. The theory was that people who bought guns in a hurry were most apt to commit crimes with them. The bill was named after James

Brady, a presidential press secretary who had been seriously wounded in an assassination attempt on President Ronald Reagan.

PROBLEMS RIGHT OFF THE BAT

All did not go well, however. Clinton put First Lady Hillary in charge of his health reform plan, and she met with tremendous resistance. Republicans argued that the plan was too expensive and would involve too much governmental interference in health care. Health insurance companies added their protests to the Republican side. Finally, the Clintons had to concede defeat, and the plan was abandoned.

Controversy also surrounded the president and the first lady's private life and business dealings. One scandal stemmed from suspicious investments that he and Hillary had made in an Arkansas real-estate development firm, the Whitewater Development Corporation. The Senate investigated the Whitewater dealings and a federal prosecutor, Kenneth Starr, was asked to look further into the matter.

Because of Clinton's liberal politics, many conservative Republicans were looking for reasons to criticize the man as well as his policies. Unfortunately for Clinton, he often provided political fuel for their efforts. Some of this fuel was provided by a lawsuit brought by a former Arkansas government employee, Paula Jones, who claimed that Clinton, while governor of Arkansas, had made unwanted advances toward her. Clinton denied the charges.

Amidst those difficulties, the Clintons were shaken by tragedy when their good friend and Hillary's longtime colleague at the Rose Law Firm, Vince Foster, committed suicide. Foster had been the Clintons' partner in the Whitewater investment deal.

The Republicans made good use of the president's personal and political problems in the 1994 congressional elections. They won enough new seats in Congress to give them a majority in the House and the Senate. It was the first time the Republicans had had control of the Congress in forty years.

On the foreign front, Bill Clinton was most influential in the Middle East. Hostilities between Arabs and Jews had had that region on the edge of war for many years. Clinton aided in securing a peace agreement between Israel and the Arab organization known as the Palestinian Liberation Organization (PLO).

In Europe Clinton also had to deal with conflict in the countries that claimed independence from Yugoslavia in the early 1990s. The president authorized aerial attacks to rescue United Nations (UN) peacekeeping troops stationed

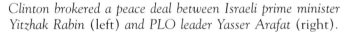

Clinton brokered a peace deal between Israeli prime minister Yitzhak Rabin (left) and PLO leader Yasser Arafat (right).

there. Then he sent a diplomatic mission into the area to
arrange a cease-fire among the warring groups. In his 1994
State of the Union address, Clinton said that he was proud
of what he had accomplished, but he was quick to point
out that there was much more work to do.

DOING WHAT HE DOES BEST

In April 1995, a young protester, Timothy McVeigh, blew
up a government building in Oklahoma City, Oklahoma,
killing 168 people. Clinton traveled to Oklahoma City and
did one of the things he does best. He gave a nationally
televised speech that showed his compassion and ability to
comfort the relatives of the victims, as well as a nervous
city. He helped the nation heal.

In 1995 the Republicans, led by Speaker of the House
Newt Gingrich, refused to approve the annual budget
presented by Clinton. They passed their own budget
request, which Clinton refused to sign. As a result, federal offices and institutions shut down for three weeks.

——————————— ✧ ———————————

In the wake of the destruction of the federal building in Oklahoma City,
Clinton traveled to the city to help calm the residents.

ACCOMPLISHMENTS OF CLINTON'S FIRST TERM

Between 1992 and 1996, during President Clinton's first four years in office, his tax increases and budget cuts helped decrease the nation's budget deficit by 60 percent. The deficit is the amount of money the government needs to borrow when the money it receives from taxes is less than the money it spends.

When Clinton took office, 7 percent of the nation's workforce did not have jobs. After four years, that number had shrunk to 5.4 percent. Ten million new jobs were created during the four-year period.

During his first term, Clinton signed into law the Family and Medical Leave Act, which requires employers to give their employees time off for illness and to tend to family matters. He witnessed the signing of the Israeli-Palestinian Declaration of Principles at the White House by Israeli prime minister Yitzhak Rabin and Palestinian leader Yasser Arafat. He signed into law the North American Free Trade Agreement, which encourages trade and investment among the United States, Canada, and Mexico. He visited Belfast, Northern Ireland, to lend his support to the peace process there. And he signed into law the Brady Bill requiring a five-day waiting period when buying a handgun.

They were—technically, anyway—out of money. During that time, Washington, D.C., was all but closed. A compromise was worked out that allowed government offices to reopen.

RUNNING FOR REELECTION

In the 1996 presidential elections, Bill Clinton once again had not one opponent but two. He ran against the Republican candidate, Senator Bob Dole of Kansas, and—again running on an independent ticket—H. Ross Perot, the Texas billionaire.

As in the 1992 elections, Perot's candidacy helped Clinton more than it helped Bob Dole. Most of Perot's

Republican Bob Dole, a World War II hero, appealed to many conservative voters but lacked Clinton's charisma and relative youth.

voters would have voted for Dole if Perot had not been running—and if that had been the case, the election might have turned out differently. In addition, voters were angered by the recent government shutdown, which they blamed on Republicans. As a result, Clinton easily won the election to a second term as president.

After his reelection, Bill Clinton stood on the steps of the Old State House in Little Rock, Arkansas, and said to his supporters, "I thank the people of my beloved state. I would not be anywhere else in the world tonight. In front of this old Capitol that has seen so much of my own life and our state's history, I thank you for staying with me for so long, for never giving up, for always knowing we could do better. . . . My fellow Americans, we have work to do."

*During his second inaugural address, Clinton urged people of all
races and backgrounds to unite as Americans.*

CHAPTER EIGHT

SECOND TERM

"It is really a potentially great thing for America that we are becoming so multiethnic at the time the world is becoming closely tied together. But it's also potentially a powder keg of problems and heartbreak and division and loss."

—Bill Clinton, remarks to the Society of Newspaper Editors, 1997

Clinton had not forgotten the passions for racial equality that he had acquired as a boy. At his second inaugural address, on January 20, 1997, he again spoke out against the divide in America caused by racial prejudice.

The divide of race has been America's constant curse. And each new wave of immigrants gives new targets to old prejudices. Prejudice and contempt, cloaked in the pretense of religious or political conviction are no different. These forces have nearly destroyed our nation in the past. They plague us still. They fuel the fanaticism of terror. And they torment the lives of millions in fractured nations all around the world. These obsessions cripple both those who hate and, of course, those who are hated, robbing both of what they might become. We cannot, we will not, succumb to the dark impulses that lurk in the far regions of the soul everywhere. We shall overcome them. And we shall replace them with the generous spirit of a people who feel at home with one another. Our rich texture of racial, religious and political diversity will be a Godsend in the twenty-first century. Great rewards will come to those who can live together, learn together, work together, forge new ties that bind together.

The second term of Clinton's administration began with the question of balancing the budget. This time, Clinton compromised with the hostile Republican Congress and got the job done.

TROUBLES CONTINUE

Clinton was still being dogged by both the Whitewater investigation and the Paula Jones case, but his problems didn't stop there. Clinton, along with Vice President Al Gore, were accused of illegal fundraising for their 1996 campaign. Both leaders maintained that all of their activities were within the letter of the law. In response, they called for reforms in the way campaigns are financed.

In the second year of Clinton's second term, a scandal

White House intern
Monica Lewinsky (left)
stood next to Clinton
at a 1996 presidential
campaign event.
─────────── ✧

came close to bringing down Clinton's entire presidency. A young White House intern, Monica Lewinsky, claimed to have had a sexual relationship with the president in the Oval Office. When testifying in court in the Paula Jones case on his own behalf, the Lewinsky affair was raised. President Clinton denied having a relationship with Lewinsky.

Whitewater special prosecutor Kenneth Starr shifted gears and began to investigate Lewinsky's claims. It turned out that Lewinsky could prove she was telling the truth. That meant that Clinton had lied. To make matters much worse, Clinton had lied under oath while testifying for a court. This is a crime called perjury. Clinton was also accused of trying to convince Lewinsky to lie when she was called to testify in the Paula Jones case. That too, if it were true, was a crime called obstruction of justice. Clinton settled his suit with Jones in November 1998 for $850,000, offering no apology and admitting no guilt.

Starr meanwhile sent a report to the House of

Kenneth Starr

————— ✧ —————

Representatives, contending that the president's alleged perjury and obstruction of justice could be grounds for impeachment. Bill Clinton's presidency and his legacy were likely to be forever marred by what his enemies called criminal behavior and what his friends called "marital difficulties."

Many people thought that Clinton's sexual behavior was a private matter between Clinton and his wife and that it was nobody else's business. Clinton's enemies, on the other hand, believed that Clinton's perjury and obstruction of justice were grounds to remove him from office. Because of his illegal behavior while president, Clinton became the second U.S. president to be impeached (charged by the House of Representatives with misconduct in office). The Senate went on to try President Clinton. The televised trial was held to determine whether Clinton should be removed from office.

The impeachment and trial were highly controversial because they cost a lot of tax dollars. In addition, many people felt that Clinton's crimes had little to do with politics or governing. They focused on Clinton's personal life.

To remove a president from office, two-thirds of all U.S.

U.S. senators voted on whether or not to remove Clinton from office.

senators have to vote for conviction. To force Clinton from office, many Democrats would have had to vote for a conviction. But, as expected, the Senate voted along party lines. Most Republicans voted to remove Clinton from office, and most Democrats voted to let him remain. With more Democrats in the Senate at the time, the final vote on February 12, 1999, found Clinton not guilty of the charges against him, and he remained in office.

Clinton's enemies were disappointed by the vote. They felt that the man they often called "Slick Willie" had once again gotten off the hook. Clinton's supporters were also angry. They felt that the chances of getting a conviction had been slim all along. They considered the entire impeachment process and trial to be an embarrassing waste of time and money.

Clinton's presidency had been forever changed. Even Clinton supporters had to admit that many of the good things about his presidency had become overwhelmed by the scandal.

STATE OF THE UNION

In his 1998 State of the Union address, President Clinton could report to the American people that the country's economy was booming. He hoped this good news would turn people's focus away from his impeachment and the Monica Lewinsky affair. He said:

> These are good times for America. We have more than 14 million new jobs; the lowest unemployment in 24 years; the lowest core inflation in 30 years; incomes are rising; and we have the highest homeownership in history. Crime has dropped for a record five years in a row. And the welfare rolls are at their lowest levels in 27 years. Our leadership in the world is unrivaled. Ladies and gentlemen, the state of our Union is strong.... This is the America we have begun to build; this is the America we can leave to our children—if we join together to finish the work at hand. Let us strengthen our nation for the 21st century.

ON THE FOREIGN FRONT

In August 1998, terrorists bombed the U.S. embassies in Kenya and Tanzania in Africa, killing 257 people and injuring more than 5,000. The attacks were attributed to Osama bin Laden and his al-Qaeda terrorist organization,

In his 1998 State of the Union address, Clinton tried to draw the nation's attention away from his troubled presidency by focusing on the thriving economy.

the same people who were later responsible for the September 11, 2001, attacks on the World Trade Center and the Pentagon. After the 1998 bombings, Clinton ordered air strikes on the terrorist hideouts in Afghanistan and Sudan. To this day, Clinton regrets that those strikes were not successful. If they had been, thousands of Americans' lives might have been spared on September 11, 2001.

Also in 1998, Clinton ordered the U.S. Air Force to bomb Iraq. In 1991 Iraq had invaded the small neighboring country of Kuwait. United Nations member countries, led by the United States, came to the aid of Kuwait and defeated the Iraqis in what is known as the Persian Gulf War.

CLINTON'S FOREIGN POLICY

President Clinton became more confident and effective in all aspects of leadership during his eight years as president. Nowhere was the improvement more apparent than in the field of foreign policy—how a nation deals with other nations, both friends and enemies.

The *Washington Post* wrote that during the early days of his presidency, Clinton seemed "naive" and handled foreign policy as if "he were an exchange student." Clinton, however, eventually "developed his own instincts about the world and the confidence to trust them."

Clinton looked at issues from various points of view and sought solutions that would be acceptable to all sides. In this way, he determined the best foreign policies to follow. Clinton brought tremendous goodwill to U.S.-Russian relations by befriending Russian President Boris Yeltsin. He also effectively brought together the Palestinians and Israelis for talks in the Middle East. In Northern Ireland, where Catholics and Protestants were at odds, his fine sense of compromise helped bring about peace negotiations.

Since Bill Clinton considered himself a man of peace, he agonized over the use of military force during the early days of his presidency. But he soon learned to use it appropriately. During his presidency, he ordered military interventions in Haiti, Bosnia, Kosovo, Iraq, Sudan, Somalia, and Afghanistan.

A U.S. war plane makes its way from Turkey to attack Iraq in 1998.

Iraq then agreed to allow UN personnel to inspect weapons facilities in that country, to make sure that it was not making weapons of mass destruction. It also agreed to a ban on flights over areas in the northern and southern Iraq to protect minority populations living there from a hostile Iraqi government. These no-fly zones were patrolled by planes from UN member countries. When Iraqi guns fired on planes patrolling the no-fly zones in 1998, Clinton ordered U.S. planes to bomb the gun placements.

That same year, Clinton aided in another agreement between the Israelis and the Palestinians. This one stated that, in exchange for an end to Palestinian terrorism, Israel would withdraw from areas known as the West Bank and the Gaza Strip, both claimed by the Palestinians.

PARDON ME

With their final days in the White House ahead, the Clintons began to make plans for the future. Hillary Clinton, who was an experienced lawyer and a visible part of her husband's presidency, decided to run for the U.S. Senate, and in 2000, she was elected senator for New York State.

On his last day in office, Clinton escaped a possible criminal scandal by agreeing to admit that he had given misleading testimony in the Paula Jones case. On that day, Clinton released a statement in which he admitted that he had "knowingly violated" the law when giving his false testimony.

It is also customary for U.S. presidents, on their last day in office, to pardon people facing criminal charges or to release from prison those they believe are unjustly held or who have already paid a sufficient price for their crimes.

——————————— ✧ ———————————

Hillary and Vice President Gore reenacted Hillary's January 2001 swearing in to the Senate, as Clinton and daughter Chelsea watched.

HILLARY BECOMES SENATOR

First Lady Hillary Clinton announced that she was a candidate for senator from New York State in 1999. Her opponent was to be the popular Republican mayor of New York City, Rudolph Giuliani.

The president gave a ringing endorsement to his wife's candidacy: "It would be a great thing for the country. It's very unusual to find somebody like that, who has that much knowledge and background and passion packed into one place."

Hillary's chance of winning the election received a boost when Mayor Giuliani withdrew from the race because of health and personal problems. His replacement, Rick Lazio, was not as well known and less popular.

A senator needs to have a home in the state he or she represents. Since law school, Hillary had been living in either Arkansas or Washington, D.C. The Clintons bought a home in Chappaqua, New York, about 45 miles north of New York City, so that Hillary could run for office in New York.

On November 7, 2000, Hillary Clinton won the U.S. Senate race in New York. She is the first First Lady elected to the U.S. Senate and the first woman to be elected in a statewide election in New York.

These presidential pardons often have been controversial.

Few presidential pardons have provoked the same outrage as President Clinton's pardon of fugitive billionaire Marc Rich. At the time, Rich was living in Switzerland so he wouldn't have to face criminal charges of tax evasion and other offenses in the United States. Many Americans viewed the pardon with suspicion when it was revealed that Rich's former wife, Denise Rich, was a friend of President Clinton. She had donated $450,000 to a fund to build Clinton's presidential library in Little Rock. With

—————————— ✧ ——————————

Clinton's pardon of fugitive Marc Rich raised eyebrows because of Clinton's friendship with Rich's former wife, Denise, with whom he is pictured below at a 1998 fundraiser.

this donation, it appeared as if Mrs. Rich had purchased a presidential pardon for her former husband. It was later revealed that Ehud Barak, then prime minister of Israel, had also asked Clinton to pardon Rich, because Rich had donated significant amounts of money to Israeli causes.

President Clinton had left office under yet another cloud of controversy. This left many voters and historians with a mixed view of the legacy of a talented politician who was able to bring the nation new prosperity and increased international influence.

HARLEM WELCOMES
PRESIDENT CLINTON

Clinton waved to supporters and new neighbors at a rally
welcoming him to his new office in Harlem.

CHAPTER NINE

AT HOME IN HARLEM

"I want you to know that I want to be a good neighbor . . . on the best days and the dark days, for all the people of Harlem."
—Bill Clinton

On July 30, 2001, former president Bill Clinton moved into new offices in the Harlem section of New York City. This was the first time a former president had ever conducted his business out of a predominantly African American community. His Harlem offices are on the top floor of a newly renovated fourteen-story building.

Harlem was not Clinton's first choice as the site for his offices. He had originally chosen space in the Carnegie Towers in a central area of Manhattan, which would have cost twice as much as the Harlem offices. Since a former president's office space is paid for by taxpayers' money, the price of his original choice caused another uproar.

So Clinton chose offices in Harlem instead, and a street

*Clinton enjoyed music played by fellow saxophonists at
his welcoming ceremony in Harlem.*

———————— ✧ ————————

rally welcomed him a few blocks from his new offices on
Harlem's 125th Street. The daylong party featured speeches
praising Clinton from many Harlem leaders and New York
area political leaders. Cicely Tyson, an actress and native of
Harlem, acted as mistress of ceremonies.

When Clinton finally took the podium, he promised
that he would use his new office as a base to fight world
poverty and AIDS. "What I'm going to do here is to try
to help promote economic opportunity in our backyard,
in our country and around the world," Clinton said. "I
feel like I am home."

As president, Clinton had set up federal empowerment zones, which provide federal money to some of America's poorest neighborhoods. Harlem was one of them. At the rally, Clinton told the crowd that he was proud to live in a federal empowerment zone.

Some people, such as Terry Lane, president and CEO of the Upper Manhattan Empowerment Zone, said, "It was very significant that . . . former President Clinton would have his office located here in central Harlem. His being here helps . . . the economic fiber of urban America." New York governor George Pataki spoke at the rally and proclaimed that Monday as William Jefferson Clinton Day in Harlem. Supporters chanted, "We Want Bill."

But not everyone at the rally was a supporter. A small group of protesters chanted, "Clinton go home." Members of the Black Panther Party, a group actively seeking to empower African Americans, were among the protesters. Chanting, "Whose streets? Our streets?" they said they feared that Clinton's move to Harlem would force

──────── ✧

A Harlem resident showed his displeasure at Clinton's choice of office space.

rents in the neighborhood to go up, thus forcing poor African Americans to move out.

"I want to make sure I'm a good neighbor in Harlem. I'm glad the property values are going up, but I don't want the small business people to be run out because I'm coming in," Clinton said.

LUCRATIVE MEMOIRS

On August 7, 2001, the Alfred A. Knopf publishing company announced that it would publish Bill Clinton's autobiography in 2003 and that the former president was being paid $10 million for his efforts. The offer bested the $8-million book contract that Senator Hillary Clinton had signed only a few weeks before. Senator Clinton's autobiography was published by Simon & Schuster.

"President Clinton is one of the dominant figures on the global stage," Sonny Mehta, president and editor in chief of Knopf, said. "He has lived an extraordinary life, and he has a great story to tell. His memoir, one of the most widely anticipated books in memory, will be a thorough and candid telling of his life, with a primary focus on the White House years." There can be nothing better for the potential sales of a book than the public feeling that the author has some explaining to do.

In writing his $10 million biography, Clinton doesn't have to rely on his memory, at least when writing about his eight years in the White House. That's because he kept an ongoing, recorded diary of those years. He regularly spoke into a tape recorder to record his day-to-day impressions of the presidency. He has about eighty cassette tapes from that period.

CHELSEA CLINTON: A NEW FORCE

Chelsea Clinton was twelve years old when her father became president of the United States. Her parents tried to keep the media away from her so that her privacy could be protected. In Washington, D.C., Chelsea attended the Sidwell Friends School, where she was a National Merit Scholar. In 1997, protected by her Secret Service guards, she went on to Stanford University in California, majoring in history. At Stanford, no longer shielded from publicity, she found her romances appearing on the front page of national newspapers. But she accepted it all in good grace, and she maintained her reputation as a thoroughly nice person.

Chelsea was in downtown Manhattan during the terrorist attack on September 11, 2001. She wrote a well-publicized article in *Talk* magazine about her thoughts and experiences on that day.

After Stanford Chelsea attended Oxford University in England, where her father had studied as a Rhodes scholar. She received a degree in international relations there and has been hired as a consultant at a London-based company.

✧ ————————

Chelsea spent most of her teenage years in the White House, sometimes accompanying her parents on political trips abroad.

In the aftermath of the September 11 terrorist attacks, workers cleared wreckage from the World Trade Center site, known as Ground Zero.

AFTERMATH OF THE TERRORIST ATTACKS

On September 11, 2001, terrorists hijacked commercial jetliners to destroy the 110-story twin towers of the World Trade Center in New York City, killing nearly three thousand people. Another similar attack killed nearly 200 people at the Pentagon near Washington, D.C. Bill Clinton was in Australia at the time to give a speech. After the attacks, President George W. Bush, Clinton's successor, quickly sent a military cargo plane to bring Clinton home. Clinton voiced support for President Bush: "We should not be second-guessing. We should be supporting him," he said.

Back in New York, among those affected by the brutal acts were the students of two high schools a block away from the site of the towers. Both schools were evacuated quickly. "I was with my ninth-graders," said teacher Tajuana Johnson. "Some, as we were getting through the streets, noticed that there were those who weren't keeping up. They went back to help." Avoiding the billowing cloud of dust and debris, the students were moved south a few blocks, and eventually they spent the rest of the day in the gymnasium of Staten Island's Curtis High School.

The students remained displaced for months because their schools were in the "frozen zone," too close to the disaster to be safe. One of the schools had been used as a morgue during the first hours after the buildings fell.

When Bill Clinton heard about the flight of the students from the two schools closest to the disaster, he decided to pay them a visit. Clinton spoke to them on September 24, 2001, in the auditorium of a school in downtown Manhattan that had become a temporary school for the displaced students.

Visiting students whose high schools were affected by the September 11 terrorist attacks, Clinton and New York City schools chancellor Howard Levy said the "Pledge of Allegiance."

Before a room full of traumatized but ecstatic teenagers, he said: "The terrorists can only win if they can get inside our heads and hearts. They can only win if they make us afraid of going out, afraid to live, to work, to go to school—if they make us afraid of each other. In other words, the only way bin Laden can win is if we help him win. That's the most important thing I want to tell you: These people cannot win unless you give them permission. Don't do it. Keep your life."

It was an emotional moment, and many students were comforted. "When I hear him speak, I feel better. I have more confidence," said fifteen-year-old sophomore Kimberly Dotel.

Following the speech, Clinton went into the student audience with a microphone and answered questions. The students quickly proved that, despite the emotion of the moment, they were not too awed by Clinton to ask questions.

"How do you feel about not being president?" a student inquired.

"My feelings are irrelevant. I served my time and did the best I could." After pausing for the enthusiastic applause, Clinton continued, "The most important thing is for people like me not to get in the way of uniting the country."

TEAMING WITH DOLE

National crises have a way of pulling people together. Nowhere was that clearer than in the library of Georgetown University on October 31, 2001. There, having coffee and doughnuts together, were former president Bill Clinton and

Clinton and Dole's collaboration to raise money for the Families of Freedom Scholarship Fund symbolized the spirit of unity between political parties in the period after September 11.

former Senate majority leader Bob Dole, the man who had run against Clinton in the 1996 presidential election.

The pair had just agreed to endorse the Families of Freedom Scholarship Fund for the children of those killed in the September 11 terrorist attacks. They taped a 30-second television commercial together and later announced their goal was to raise $100 million for the fund. Both politicians stated that they hoped the new feelings of cooperation between Democrats and Republicans lasted beyond the time of crisis.

"I think all Americans long for a return to normalcy, you know, where you feel the security necessary to have an honest debate over issues, where there can be a genuine difference of opinion," Clinton said. "And we're not there yet."

Of the unusual cooperation between opposing political parties, Dole commented: "It's obviously not going to last forever," Dole said, "and it's important to have . . . [political] parties, different ideas, competition [but] I think there will be some fundamental changes."

"We'll all be reminded that what we have in common is still so much more important than our differences," Clinton said.

SAVING HIS LEGACY

Clinton's political opponents have continued to attack him even now that he is out of office. A few have blamed Clinton for the September 11 attacks because he failed to destroy Osama bin Laden and the al-Qaeda terrorist network when he retaliated for the attacks on U.S. embassies in East Africa in 1998. But Clinton and several of his aides are preparing ways to protect Clinton's legacy, to emphasize to the public his accomplishments.

"It's important that the president's legacy not be squandered because his own people remain silent and scattered," said Bill Richardson, Clinton's former energy secretary. "It's important that the Democratic Party not turn away from Clinton's centrist legacy that brought us economic prosperity."

LIBRARY GROUNDBREAKING

On December 6, 2001, Bill Clinton himself turned over the first shovel of dirt in a former industrial section of Little Rock, Arkansas, where his presidential library would be built.

Clinton kicked off the construction of his presidential library in Little Rock.

At the groundbreaking ceremony, Clinton read a letter, written years before to a friend by a pregnant woman who had just lost her husband in a car accident. The letter, in part, read: "It seemed almost unbearable at the time, but you see I am six months pregnant and the thought of our baby keeps me going and really gives me the whole world before me." The letter had been written by Clinton's mother just a few months before he was born.

After reading the letter, Clinton said, "I hope I didn't let her down." And, with the combination of accomplishment and scandal that was the Clinton presidency—and life—it was a difficult question to answer.

Since 2001 Clinton has busied himself giving speeches around the world. He and Bob Dole appeared on the television show *60 Minutes* in 2003 to debate public issues. Since he is still a relatively young man, Clinton may sometime in the future become involved in politics again.

Timeline

1946 William Jefferson Blythe IV is born in Hope, Arkansas, on August 19.

1948 At the age of two, Bill is sent to live with his grandparents, who also reside in Hope, while his mother, Virginia Blythe, studies to be a nurse anesthetist in New Orleans.

1950 Bill's mother marries Roger Clinton, a car salesman.

1953 Bill and his mother and stepfather move to Hot Springs, Arkansas.

1960 Bill is a high school honor student and plays saxophone in a jazz band.

1962 Bill's last name is legally changed to Clinton.

1963 On a visit to the White House as part of the American Legion's Boys Nation, Bill shakes hands with President John F. Kennedy and decides to go into politics.

1964 Bill enters Georgetown University in Washington, D.C. He is elected president of his freshman class.

1966 Bill helps in Judge Frank Holt's campaign for Arkansas governor. Bill becomes an aide to Arkansas senator William J. Fulbright.

1968 Bill graduates from Georgetown University with a degree in international affairs. Bill attends Oxford University in England on a Rhodes Scholarship.

1969 Clinton becomes an anti-Vietnam War organizer in England.

1970 Clinton enters Yale Law School, in New Haven, Connecticut.

1972 Clinton directs the Texas campaign of Democratic presidential nominee George S. McGovern.

1973 Clinton receives his law degree from Yale. He returns to his home state and teaches law at the University of Arkansas.

1974   Clinton formally begins his political career by running for the U.S. House of Representatives. He loses but earns more votes than any previous Democrat.

1975   Clinton marries Hillary Rodham on October 11.

1976   Clinton is elected Arkansas attorney general. He also manages the Arkansas campaign of Democratic presidential candidate Jimmy Carter.

1978   Clinton is elected governor of Arkansas at age 32.

1980   Chelsea Clinton is born on February 27. Clinton seeks reelection as governor and loses to Frank D. White.

1982   Clinton is reelected as governor of Arkansas.

1984   Clinton is elected to a third term as governor. He delivers a speech at the Democratic National Convention in San Francisco, California.

1986   Clinton is elected to a fourth term as governor. He becomes chair of the National Governors Association.

1988   Clinton gives the nominating speech for presidential candidate Michael Dukakis at the Democratic National Convention in Atlanta, Georgia.

1990   Clinton is elected to a fifth term as Arkansas governor.

1991   Clinton announces that he is a candidate for president of the United States.

1992   Clinton is elected president of the United States, defeating incumbent George H. W. Bush.

1993   Clinton signs the Family and Medical Leave Act. He witnesses the signing, by Israeli prime minister Yitzhak Rabin and Palestinian leader Yasser Arafat, of the Israeli-Palestinian Declaration of Principles at the White House. He signs into law the Brady Bill. He signs the North American Free Trade Agreement.

1995 Clinton visits Belfast, Northern Ireland, the scene of violence between Catholics and Protestants, to support the peace process there.

1996 Clinton is reelected as president of the United States, defeating Bob Dole.

1998 Clinton is impeached on charges of perjury and obstruction of justice.

1999 Clinton is found not guilty of the impeachment charges against him at the Senate trial.

2001 Clinton's term as president ends. The former president moves into offices in the predominantly African American Harlem section of New York City. Clinton signs a record $10-million book contract to write the story of his life.

2003 Clinton faces Bob Dole for weekly discussions of political issues on the television show *60 Minutes*.

Source Notes

7 "Bill Clinton: First Inaugural Address," *Bartleby.com,* January 21, 1993, <http://www.bartleby.com/124/pres64.html> (April 22, 2003).

7–8 Ibid.

9 Charles F. Allen and Jonathan Portis, *The Comeback Kid: The Life and Career of Bill Clinton* (New York: Birch Lane Press, 1992), 5.

10 David Maraniss, *First in His Class: A Biography of Bill Clinton* (New York: Simon & Schuster, 1995), 32.

11 Ibid., 66.

12 Don Baer, "Man-Child in Politics Land," *U.S. News & World Report,* October 14, 1991, 40.

13 Allen and Portis, 17–18.

13 Maraniss, 15.

15 Ibid., 17.

15 Ibid., 84.

17 George Carpozi Jr., *Clinton Confidential: The Climb to Power* (Del Mar, CA: Emery Dalton Books, 1995), 28.

18 Allen and Portis, 23.

20 Maraniss, 78.

21 Ibid., 91.

27 Allen and Portis, 31.

27 "The Rhodes Scholarships," *"The Rhodes Scholarship Trust,* July 2002, <http://www.rhodesscholar.org> (June 11, 2003).

28 Maraniss, 124.

28–29 Ibid.

29 Allen and Portis, 31.

29 Ibid.

36 Maraniss, 247.

36 Allen and Portis, 34.

45 Ibid., 82.

53 Maraniss, 41.

57 Allen and Portis, 82.

59 "Announcement Speech, Old State House, Little Rock, Arkansas," *SunSITE*, October 3, 1991, <http://sunsite.tus.ac.jp/pub/academic/political-science/speeches/clinton.dir/c27.txt> (November 18, 2002).

60 Ibid.

62 Eleanor Clift, "Political Ambitions, Personal Choices," *Newsweek,* March 9, 1992, 36.

64 Ibid.

67 Allen and Portis, 268.

73 Howard Fineman with Bill Turque, "Hail and Farewell," *Newsweek,* November 18, 1996, 8.

75 "President William Jefferson Clinton Excerpts from Remarks by the President to the Annual Meeting of the American Society of Newspaper Editors," *The American Society of Newspaper Editors*, April 10, 1997, <http://clinton4.nara.gov/textonly/initiatives/OneAmerica/19970610–1292.html> (November 20, 2002).

75–76 "Bill Clinton's Second Inaugural Address," *School for Champions,* January 20, 1997, <http://www.school-forchampions.com/speeches/clinton_inaugural.htm> (November 16, 2002).

80 "President Bill Clinton's State of the Union Address," *CNN All Politics*, n.d., <http://www.cnn.com/allpolitics/1998/01/27/sotu/transcripts/clinton> (November 15, 2002).

82 Steven Mufson and John F. Harris, "Novice Became Confident Diplomat on World Stage," *Washington Post,* January 15, 2001, A3.

82 Ibid.

85 Dale McFeatters, "President Clinton Is Definitely Back," *Abilene Reporter-News,* July 27, 1999, A1.

89 "Harlem Street Jam Welcomes Clinton to New Office," *CNN.com,* July 31, 2002, <http://www.cnn.com/ allpolitics/1998/01/27/sotu/ transcripts/clinton> (July 31, 2001).

90 Ibid.

91 Ibid.

91 Ibid.

92 Ibid.

92 Linton Weeks, "Clinton to Reap Over $10 Million for His Memoirs," *Washington Post,* August 7, 2001, A1.

94 Michael Grunwald, "Clinton Stays at Spotlight's Edge," *Washington Post,* September 29, 2001, A4.

94–95 Michael Hirsch, "Displaced Schools and Hosts Learn New Meaning of Sharing," *New York Teacher,* October 10, 2001, 5.

96 Nick Chiles, "Clinton: Terrorists Will Win if We Fear," *Newsday,* September 25, 2001, 9.

96 Ibid.

96 Ibid.

97–98 Susan Page, "Clinton and Dole Join Together for Charity Ad," *USA Today,* October 31, 2001, A7.

98 Ibid.

98 Ibid.

98 Richard L. Berke, "Clinton and Aides Lay Plans to Repair a Battered Image," *New York Times,* December 21, 2001, A3.

99 John F. Harris, "Groundbreaking for a Library and a Legacy," *Washington Post,* December 6, 2001, A9.

99 Ibid.

SELECTED BIBLIOGRAPHY

Allen, Charles F., and Jonathan Portis. *The Comeback Kid: The Life and Career of Bill Clinton.* New York: Birch Lane Press, 1992.

Baer, Don. "Man-Child in Politics Land." *U.S. News & World Report,* October 14, 1991, 40.

Berke, Richard L. "Clinton and Aides Lay Plans to Repair a Battered Image." *New York Times,* December 21, 2001, A3.

"Bill's Scottish Fans Get Earful from Anti-Israel Protesters." *New York Post,* December 11, 2001, 26.

Blomquist, Brian. "Top Court Officially Boots Bill from Lawyer List." *New York Post,* November 14, 2001, 35.

"Bubba Gives up Challenge to High Court Disbarment." *New York Post,* November 10, 2001, 3.

Carpozi, George Jr. *Clinton Confidential: The Climb to Power.* Del Mar, CA: Emery Dalton Books, 1995.

Chiles, Nick. "Clinton: Terrorists Will Win if We Fear." *Newsday,* September 25, 2001, 9.

Clift, Eleanor. "Political Ambitions, Personal Choices." *Newsweek,* March 9, 1992, 36.

"Clinton Ran Rich Pardon by Barak." *Washington Post,* August 22, 2001, A5.

Fineman, Howard, with Bill Turque, "Hail and Farewell." *Newsweek,* November 18, 1996, 8.

Gellman, Barton. "The Covert Hunt for Bin Laden: Broad Effort Launched After '98 Attacks." *The Washington Post,* December 19, 2001, A6.

Gest, Emily. "Chelsea Toast of Town." *Daily News,* January 6, 2002, 25.

Grunwald, Michael. "Clinton Stays at Spotlight's Edge." *Washington Post,* September 29, 2001, A4.

Harris, John F. "Groundbreaking for a Library and a Legacy." *Washington Post,* December 6, 2001, A9.

Maraniss, David. *First in His Class: A Biography of Bill Clinton.* New York: Simon & Schuster, 1995.

McFeatters, Dale. "President Clinton Is Definitely Back." *Abilene Reporter-News,* July 27, 1999, A1.

Morris, Dick. "Non-War on Terror: Bill Had Other Priorities." *New York Post,* December 26, 2001, 31.

Page, Susan. "Clinton and Dole Join Together for Charity Ad." *USA Today,* October 31, 2001, A7.

Roth, Katherine. "Clinton's Harlem Neighbors Mixed about Arrival." Associated Press dispatch, July 21, 2001.

Ruddy, Christopher, and Carl Limbacher, Jr., eds. *Bitter Legacy.* West Palm Beach, FL: NewsMax.com, 2001.

Rush, George, and Joanna Molloy. "Bill's Book Will Be a Tale of the Tapes." *Daily News,* October 4, 2001, 50.

Watson, Kevin H. *The Clinton Record.* Bellevue, WA: Merril Press, 1996.

Weeks, Linton. "Clinton to Reap Over $10 Million for His Memoirs." *Washington Post,* August 7, 2001, A1.

FURTHER READING AND WEBSITES

American Presidents. <http://ap.beta.polardesign.com/history/billclinton/biography/lifebrief.common.shtml>. This site provides biographies of Bill and Hillary Clinton, introduces staff in Clinton's administrations, and outlines events from his years in office.

Clinton Presidential Center. <http://www.clintonpresidentialcenter.com/index.html>. This website monitors the progress of the Clinton Presidential Center in Little Rock, Arkansas, and offers a look at Clinton's life and presidential legacy.

Cwiklik, Robert. *Bill Clinton: President of the '90s.* Brookfield, CT: The Millbrook Press, 1997.

Di Piazza, Domenica. *Arkansas.* Minneapolis: Lerner Publications Company, 2002.

Galt, Margot Fortunato. *Stop This War! American Protest of the Conflict in Vietnam.* Minneapolis: Lerner Publications Company, 2000.

Kelly, Michael. *Bill Clinton.* Philadelphia: Chelsea House, 1999.

Kent, Zachary. *William Jefferson Clinton.* Danbury, CT: Children's Press, 1994.

Landau, Elaine. *Bill Clinton and His Presidency.* New York: Franklin Watts, 1997.

Levy, Debbie. *The Vietnam War.* Minneapolis: Lerner Publications Company, 2004.

Senator Hillary Rodham Clinton: Online Office. <http://clinton. senate.gov/>. Hillary Clinton's senatorial website provides her biography, as well as updates about her work as a U.S. senator for New York.

The White House. <http://www.whitehouse.gov/history/presidents/ bc42.html>. The White House's website offers a biography of Bill Clinton.

INDEX

Afghanistan, U.S. air strikes on, 81, 82
African Americans, 10, 24, 89; view of
    Clinton, 50, 91
alcoholism, 11–12, 21
Aller, Frank, 33
Alpha Phi Omega, 19
alternative military service, 31
American Legion's Boys Nation, 13–14,
    17
Arafat, Yasser, 69, 71
Arkansas, 48; public image of, 15, 60;
    schools in, 48, 51, 52; senator from,
    15
Arkansas Advocates for Children and
    Families, 52
Arkansas Boys State, 13
Arkansas Education Standards
    Committee, 52
Arkansas Home Instruction for
    Preschool Youth, 52

Baker, Bobby, 29
Barak, Ehud, 87
Black Panther Party, 91–92
Blythe, Virginia. *See* Clinton, Virginia
    Blythe
Blythe, William Jefferson (father), 9, 99
Blythe, William Jefferson IV. *See*
    Clinton, Bill (William Jefferson)
Brady Bill, 67–68, 71
Brady, James, 67–68
Bush, George H. W., 57, 61, 62, 65
Bush, George W., 94

Camp Robinson, 13
Carson, Johnny, 56–57
Carter, Jimmy, 45–46, 49
Castro, Fidel, 49
Central Intelligence Agency (CIA), 57
civil rights, 22, 23–24
Clinton, Bill (William Jefferson):
    achievements of, 46, 69, 71, 80, 98;

athletics, 22, 29; attorney general of
    Arkansas, 45–46; autobiography of,
    92; birth and childhood, 9–15;
    college years, 17–25; criticism of, 47,
    50, 68, 98; and the draft, 30, 31, 47;
    early interest in politics, 13–15; early
    jobs, 17, 25; foreign policy of,
    69–70, 82; in fraternity, 19;
    fundraising, 76, 86–87; governor of
    Arkansas, 47–48, 49, 51, 52, 59–60;
    graduation from college, 24–25;
    grandparents of, 10; in Harlem,
    89–92; and Hillary Rodham, 36,
    38–39, 43, 54, 64, 78, 84;
    impeachment of, 78–80; and
    marijuana, 29; military interventions
    ordered by, 82; name of, 9, 10, 13;
    at Oxford University, 29, 32–33;
    personality of, 10, 18, 19, 28–29, 38,
    40, 57; political campaigning for
    others, 19–20, 25, 35, 38, 45–46;
    political philosophy of, 7–8, 45, 48,
    51, 55, 67, 68, 75–76; presidential
    library of, 86, 98–99; presidential
    pardons of, 84, 86–87; and racial
    equality, 10, 40, 50, 75–76; and
    religion, 10–11; runs for Congress,
    40–41, 42–43; saxophone player, 11,
    13, 44, 57, 90; and September 11
    attacks, 94–98; sexual scandals, 54,
    63–64, 68, 77–78; as a student, 17,
    31–35, 38, 39; in student
    government, 18–19, 20; and taxes,
    48, 63, 67, 71; as a teacher, 40; and
    terrorism, 70, 80–81, 83; on *The
    Tonight Show,* 56–57; and Vietnam
    War, 20, 22, 23, 31–32, 34; and
    Whitewater investigation, 68, 76, 77;
    at Yale, 35–36, 38, 39
Clinton, Chelsea Victoria (daughter),
    48–49, 50, 55, 84, 93
Clinton, Hillary Rodham (wife), 36,

37, 38, 39, 43, 46, 47, 48–49, 50,
51, 52, 53–54, 64, 84; autobiography
of, 92; and health reform, 68; as a
lawyer, 41–42, 47, 51; as First Lady
of Arkansas, 52; meets Bill, 35–36;
name of, 43, 49, 50; personality of,
38, 42; as senator, 85
Clinton, Roger (stepfather), 9–10, 21;
and alcoholism, 11–12, 21; nickname
of, 9
Clinton, Roger Jr. (brother), 10, 12,
21, 53–54
Clinton, Virginia Blythe (mother),
9–10, 12–13, 21, 29–30, 53–54, 60,
99; relations with Hillary, 43
Cold War, 62
Communist countries, 33–34
Congress, Democratic controlled, 67
Congress, Republican controlled, 69,
70, 76
Cuban refugees, 49

Democratic National Conventions,
Clinton at: 1984, 51, 53; 1988,
55–56; 1992, 61
Dole, Robert (Bob), 72–73, 97–98
Dotel, Kimberly, 96
draft, military, 20, 22–23, 30, 31;
evasion of, 31
Duffey, Joseph D., 35
Dukakis, Michael, 55–56, 57, 62

economy, national, 63, 67, 80, 98
education, 45, 48, 51, 52, 55

Families of Freedom Scholarship Fund,
97
Fayetteville, Arkansas, 43
federal empowerment zones, 91
Flowers, Gennifer, 63–64
foreign policy, 69–70, 81, 82, 83
Foster, Vince, 68–69

Fulbright, J. William, 15, 17, 22, 25
Fulbright scholarships, 15

Gaza Strip, 83
Georgetown University, 17, 19, 21, 22
Gingrich, Newt, 70
Giuliani, Rudolph, 85
Gore, Al Jr., 61, 62, 64–65, 76, 84
guns, laws about, 67–68, 71

Harlem, New York, 89–92
health care, 63, 68
Holt, Frank, 19–20
Holt, Lyda, 19, 20
Hope, Arkansas, 9
Hot Springs, Arkansas, 10

impeachment, 41; Clinton and, 77–80;
Nixon and, 41–42
international relations, 69–70
Iraq, 81, 82, 83
Israel, 69, 82, 83, 87
Israeli-Palestinian Declaration of
Principles, 71

Johnson, Tajuana, 94–95
Jones, Paula: case against Clinton by,
68, 76, 77, 84

Kennedy, John F., 7, 14, 23–24
Kennedy, Robert F.: assassination of,
23–24
Kenya, U.S. embassy in, 80–81
King, Martin Luther Jr.: assassination
of, 23–24
Kuwait, 81

Laden, Osama bin, 80–81, 96
Lazio, Rick, 85
Legal Service Corporation: Arkansas's,
46
Levy, Howard, 95

Lewinsky, Monica, 77
Little Rock, Arkansas, 13, 48; Old State
   House in, 46–47, 60, 73; presidential
   library in, 98–99

McGovern, George, 38–39
McVeigh, Timothy, 70
Mehta, Sonny, 92
Middle East, tensions in, 69, 82
Mondale, Walter, 51
moot court, 38

NASA (National Aeronautics and Space
   Administration), 37
National Governors Association (NGA),
   54–55
National Honor Society, 17, 37
National Merit Scholarship, 17
Nixon, Richard, 22, 38; impeachment
   case against, 41–42
North American Free Trade Agreement
   (NAFTA), 71
Northern Ireland, 71, 82
nuclear weapons, 62

obstruction of justice, 77
Oklahoma City bombing, 70
Oxford University, 25, 26–28, 29, 30,
   93; Clinton at, 29, 30

Palestinian Liberation Organization
   (PLO), 69
Palestinians, 69, 71, 83
Park Place Baptist Church, 11
peace, 69, 71, 82, 83
Pentagon, attack on, 80–81
perjury, 77
Perot, H. Ross, 61, 63, 65, 72–73
Persian Gulf War, 81
presidential elections: 1992, 59–65;
   1996, 72–73, 97
presidential library, 86, 98–99

presidential pardons, 84, 86–87
presidents, age of, 7

al-Qaeda, 80–81, 98
Quayle, Dan, 65

Rabin, Yitzhak, 69, 71
racism and racial equality, 10, 40,
   75–76
Reagan, Ronald, 68
Rhodes, Cecil J., 27–28
Rhodes Scholarship, 22, 33; criteria for,
   27–28
Rich, Marc and Denise, 86–87
Richardson, Bill, 98
Rodham, Hillary. *See* Clinton, Hillary
   Rodham
Rose Law Firm, 51
ROTC (Reserve Officer Training
   Corps), 31, 34
Russia, 82

September 11, 2001, 81, 94; aftermath
   of, 94–98
Soviet Union, 33, 62
S.S. *United States,* 28
Starr, Kenneth, 77–78
Sudan, U.S. air strikes on, 81, 82

Talbott, Strobe, 33
Tanzania, U.S. embassy in, 80–81
Taylor, Donna, 10
terrorism, 70, 80–81, 83, 94, 96, 98
Tonight Show, The, 56–57
Truman, Harry, 53
Tyson, Cicely, 90

United Nations, 81, 83
University of Arkansas Law School, 31,
   34; Bill Clinton teaches at, 40;
   Hillary Clinton teaches at, 42
U.S. Capitol, 6

U.S. embassies, attacks on, 80–81, 98

Vietnam Moratorium Committee,
  31–32
Vietnam War, 20, 22, 23; opposition
  to, 20, 22, 29, 31–32, 62

Washington, D.C., 17, 24
Watergate Scandal, 41–42
West Bank, 83
White, Frank, 49, 50, 51
Whitewater Development Corporation,
  68
Williams, Edgar, 29
World Trade Center, attacks on, 81, 94
Wright, Lindsey & Jennings, law firm
  of, 50

Yale Law School, 34, 36; Bill Clinton
  at, 35–36, 38, 39
Yeltsin, Boris, 82
Yugoslavia, UN peacekeeping force in,
  69–70

ABOUT THE AUTHOR

Michael Benson is the author of nineteen books, including the biographies *Malcolm X* and *Gloria Estefan*. Originally from Rochester, New York, Benson earned a B.A. in communication arts at Hofstra University. He is the former editor of *The Military Technical Journal* and *Fight Game* magazines. He lives in Brooklyn with his wife, daughter, and son.

————— ✧ —————

PHOTO ACKNOWLEDGMENTS